FUN FACT FILE: US HISTORY!

20 FUN FACTS ABOUT THE US CONSTITUTION

By Therese Shea

Gareth Stevens
Publishing

Please visit our website, www.garethstevens.com. For a free color catalog of all our high-quality books, call toll free 1-800-542-2595 or fax 1-877-542-2596.

Library of Congress Cataloging-in-Publication Data

Shea, Therese.
20 fun facts about the US Constitution / by Therese Shea.
   p. cm. — (Fun fact file: US history)
Includes index.
ISBN 978-1-4339-9199-8 (pbk.)
ISBN 978-1-4339-9200-1 (6-pack)
ISBN 978-1-4339-9198-1 (library binding)
1. Constitutional law—United States—Juvenile literature. 2. Constitutional history—United States—Juvenile literature. I. Shea, Therese. II. Title.
KF4550.Z9 S24 2014
342.73'029—dc23

First Edition

Published in 2014 by
Gareth Stevens Publishing
111 East 14th Street, Suite 349
New York, NY 10003

Copyright © 2014 Gareth Stevens Publishing

Designer: Sarah Liddell
Editor: Greg Roza

Photo credits: Cover, p. 1 JustASC/Shutterstock.com; p. 5 Steve McAlister/Photographer's Choice/Getty Images; p. 6 MPI/Stringer/Archive Photos/Getty Images; pp. 7 (Madison and Henry), 8 (Adams and Jefferson), 9 Stock Montage/Contributor/Archive Photos/ Getty Images; p. 10 photo courtesy of Wikimedia Commons, Map of territorial growth 1775.svg; pp. 11, 25 John Parrot/Stocktrek Images/Getty Images; p. 12 Ken Cave/ Shutterstock.com; p. 13 Buyenlarge/Contributor/Archive Photos/Getty Images; p. 14 photo courtesy of Wikimedia Commons, New York City Hall 1789b.jpg; p. 15 Medford Taylor/ National Geographic/Getty Images; pp. 16, 20 Photri Images/Superstock/Getty Images; p. 19 Underwood Archives/Contributor/Archive Photos/Getty Images; p. 21 Fuse/ Getty Images; p. 22 AFP/Handout/AFP/Getty Images; p. 23 Alex Wong/Staff/Getty Images News/Getty Images; p. 24 jamesbenet/E+/Getty Images; p. 26 Superstock/Superstock/ Getty Images; p. 27 Design Pics/Don Hammond/Getty Images; p. 29 Sean Locke/E+/ Getty Images.

Printed in the United States of America

CPSIA compliance information: Batch #CS13GS: For further information contact Gareth Stevens, New York, New York at 1-800-542-2595.

Contents

Words in the glossary appear in **bold** type the first time they are used in the text.

The Living Document

The country you know as the United States might not have endured without its **Constitution**. This **document** is more than just a piece of paper from the past.

Today, the US Constitution is at work in the presidency, Congress, and **federal** court system. It guarantees rights that citizens of many other countries don't have, such as the freedom to speak out against injustice. And though it doesn't happen often, **amendments** can be added to the Constitution, which continues the Founding Fathers' work of making "a more perfect Union."

The Preamble

We the People of the United States, in Order to form a more perfect Union, establish Justice, insure domestic Tranquility, provide for the common defense, promote the general Welfare, and secure the Blessings of Liberty to ourselves and our Posterity, do ordain and establish this Constitution for the United States of America.

Rewrite!

The US Constitution wasn't the first American constitution.

During the **American Revolution**, the Founding Fathers wrote the **Articles of Confederation**. Under this constitution, the federal government was weak. The country was helpless to defend itself— and it didn't have any money! Each state cared more about protecting its own interests than a united nation.

ARTICLES
OF
Confederation
AND
Perpetual Union
BETWEEN THE
STATES
OF
NEW-HAMPSHIRE, MASSACHUSETTS-BAY, RHODE-ISLAND AND PROVIDENCE PLANTATIONS, CONNECTICUT, NEW-YORK, NEW-JERSEY, PENNSYLVANIA, DELAWARE, MARYLAND, VIRGINIA, NORTH-CAROLINA, SOUTH-CAROLINA AND GEORGIA.

LANCASTER:
FRANCIS BAILEY.
M.DCC,LXXVII.

The Articles of Confederation went into effect in 1781 but was replaced by the US Constitution in 1789.

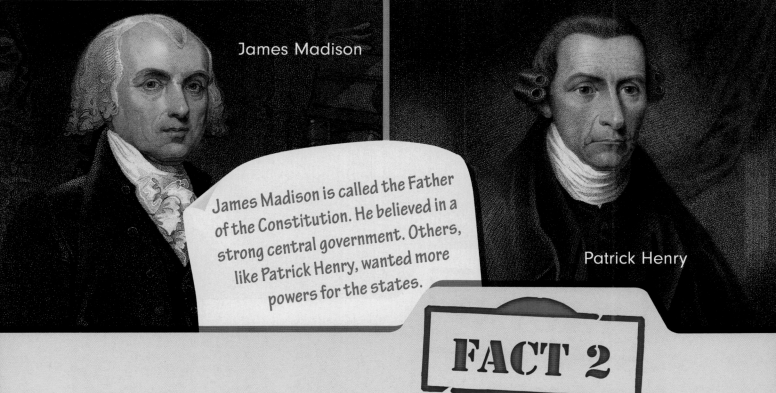

James Madison

Patrick Henry

James Madison is called the Father of the Constitution. He believed in a strong central government. Others, like Patrick Henry, wanted more powers for the states.

FACT 2

The US Constitution had a lot of enemies at first.

The Constitutional **Convention** began in 1787. Rather than changing the Articles of Confederation, a new constitution was written. Many, including war hero Patrick Henry, opposed the new document for creating a federal government that was too powerful. Henry said he "smelt a rat"!

7

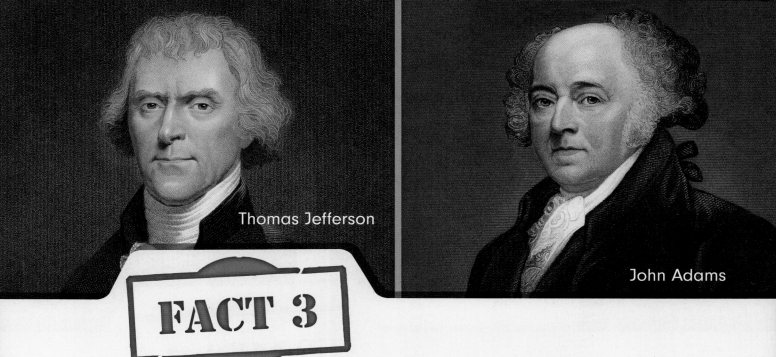

Thomas Jefferson

John Adams

FACT 3

Thomas Jefferson and John Adams weren't at the Constitutional Convention.

Despite being two of the most famous Founding Fathers, neither Thomas Jefferson nor John Adams was at the Constitutional Convention. Jefferson was a US **ambassador** in France at the time, and Adams was an ambassador in England. They never signed the Constitution.

Benjamin Franklin was the oldest person to sign the Constitution.

Benjamin Franklin was 81 years old at the Constitutional Convention. He was carried to each meeting in a chair—by prisoners from a nearby jail! Franklin wrote a speech encouraging others to support the document. Another **representative** gave the speech for him.

Benjamin Franklin

The youngest person to sign the Constitution was 26-year-old Jonathan Dayton of New Jersey.

Rhode Island finally approved the Constitution almost 2 years after it became law.

After the Constitution was approved by the convention, nine of the 13 US states needed to **ratify** it. In 1788, New Hampshire was the ninth to do so. Rhode Island, suspicious of the stronger federal government, was the last of the original 13 states to ratify it in 1790.

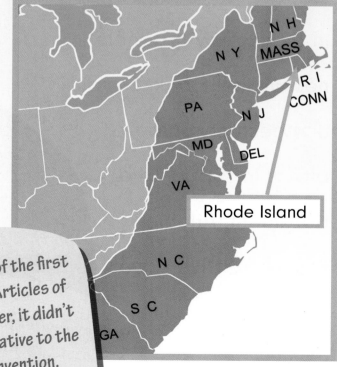

Rhode Island

Rhode Island was one of the first states to ratify the Articles of Confederation. However, it didn't even send a representative to the Constitutional Convention.

George Washington

FACT 6

There was no US president or Supreme Court before the Constitution.

Under the Articles of Confederation, the only governing body was Congress, and it got little accomplished. The new Constitution created three branches of government. Each has responsibilities and limits the others' powers. This is called the system of checks and balances.

It was important to the Founding Fathers that the president and the rest of the federal government didn't hold too much power, as a king or queen did.

FACT 7

Before the Constitution, many states made their own money.

The Articles of Confederation gave the states a lot of powers, including the right to make their own money. Congress had its own money, too. Under the Constitution, only the currency made by the federal government has value in the United States.

Besides bringing the nation one kind of money, Congress had the right to raise money through taxes under the Constitution.

Under the Articles of Confederation, Congress had the power to make war—but it could not raise an army.

The Constitution allowed for a national army, something the Articles hadn't. Some Americans had been fearful an army could be used against citizens. One representative suggested the army be small. Others pointed out enemy countries would have to shrink their armies, too!

FACT 9

The first Congress under the Constitution was held in New York City in 1789.

The Constitution laid out the framework for the government, but the job wasn't always clear or easy. After Congress's first year in 1789, representatives still hadn't agreed where the permanent federal government should be. One-third of the Senate quit in the 1790s!

The first US Congress met at Federal Hall, shown here. Today a new building—Federal Hall National Memorial—stands in its place.

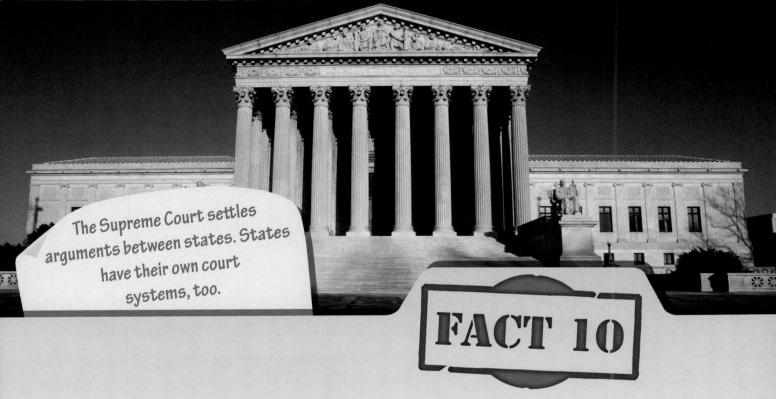

The Supreme Court settles arguments between states. States have their own court systems, too.

FACT 10

The Constitution created the Supreme Court but didn't say how many justices there should be.

Though the Constitution names the position of Chief Justice, it doesn't set the number of justices on the Supreme Court. The first court had six judges in all, but this number has changed several times. In 1869, a law fixed the number at nine.

FACT 11

The Bill of Rights originally had 12 amendments.

Some states, such as New York and Virginia, only ratified the Constitution with the promise that a bill of rights would be added. They worried the federal government would deny them certain freedoms. By 1791, 10 of 12 suggested amendments had been ratified—our Bill of Rights.

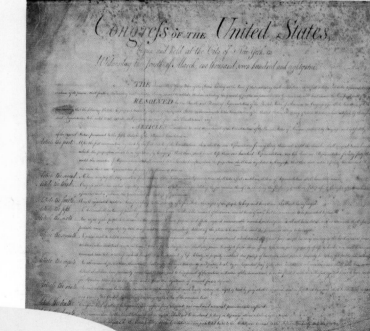

The original Bill of Rights, shown here, was introduced to Congress by James Madison in 1789.

Breakdown of the US Constitution

Preamble—purpose of the document

Article 1—establishes the legislative branch

Article 2—establishes the executive branch

Article 3—establishes the judicial branch

Article 4—outlines state powers

Article 5—describes the amendment process

Article 6—declares the Constitution the supreme law

Article 7—details the ratification process

The Bill of Rights and other amendments

The Bill of Rights

First Amendment: freedoms of religion, speech, press, assembly, and petitions

Second Amendment: right to bear arms

Third Amendment: right to refuse to house soldiers

Fourth Amendment: rights involving searches and arrests

Fifth Amendment: rights in criminal cases

Sixth Amendment: right to a fair trial

Seventh Amendment: rights in civil cases

Eighth Amendment: bail, fines, punishment

Ninth Amendment: rights of the people not otherwise stated

Tenth Amendment: states' rights

The Bill of Rights deals with some of our basic rights. Read the full text online or at the library.

At first, only white men who owned property could vote! Women got the right to vote in 1920 from the Nineteenth Amendment.

VOTES FOR WOME

FACT 12

The Bill of Rights originally affected only a small percent of the US population.

At first, the Bill of Rights didn't apply to most people living in the United States. About 20 percent of the American population was slaves. African Americans got the right to vote in 1870 through the Fifteenth Amendment. Native Americans weren't considered US citizens until 1924!

FACT 13

There are two ways that an amendment can be proposed. One has never been used in US history.

To start the amendment process, two-thirds of the Senate and two-thirds of the House of Representatives need to support it. A second proposal method requires two-thirds of the state legislatures to request a national constitutional convention. This has never happened!

The amendment process is outlined in Article V (5) of the Constitution. It was designed so that only the most important changes would pass.

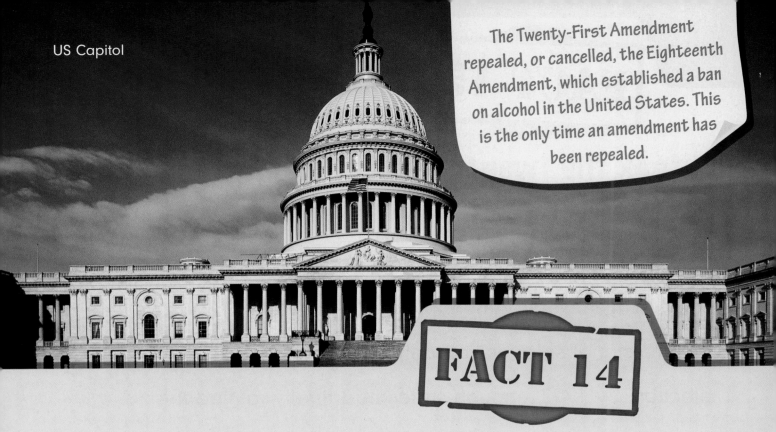

US Capitol

The Twenty-First Amendment repealed, or cancelled, the Eighteenth Amendment, which established a ban on alcohol in the United States. This is the only time an amendment has been repealed.

FACT 14

More than 11,000 constitutional amendments have been considered by Congress.

After the amendment proposal passes, it's up to the states. For ratification of an amendment, three-fourths of the states (or special state conventions) must agree to it. Most don't get that far. The process is so tough that only 27 out of more than 11,000 amendments have passed.

FACT 15

It took the Twenty-Seventh Amendment 202 years to pass!

Some amendment proposals don't have **expiration** dates. The Twenty-Seventh Amendment—proposed in 1789—says that congressional salaries can only change after the following election. By 1992, enough states had finally ratified the amendment, making it a law 202 years after it was first proposed!

FACT 16

The United States has the shortest constitution in the world.

The Constitution has 4,543 words without its amendments. That might not sound short, but it's actually the shortest constitution in the world! It's also one of the oldest constitutions. The United States has the oldest single-document constitution.

An original copy of the Constitution can be found in the National Archives in Washington, DC. There are four pages in all.

FACT 17

There are misspellings in the Constitution.

"Pennsylvania" is spelled "Pensylvania" in the Constitution.

You may see the word "chuse" instead of "choose" as well.

This is how some people spelled these words at the time.

However, in Article 1, the writer uses "it's" when he should have written "its."

The writer of the Constitution was a man named Jacob Shallus. He was paid $30 to write out the words agreed upon at the convention.

The word "democracy" isn't in the Constitution.

Benjamin Franklin

Did you know the United States isn't a true democracy? The word can't be found in the Constitution. In a democracy, citizens directly vote on laws. The United States is a republic. In a republic, people elect representatives to make decisions.

According to a story, a woman approached Benjamin Franklin at the end of the convention and asked what kind of government the representatives had created. Franklin replied, "A republic, if you can keep it."

FACT 19

Thanksgiving Day was originally a day of thanks for the Constitution and new government.

We think of Pilgrims and Native Americans when we think of Thanksgiving, but the first American Thanksgiving was meant to honor something else. In 1789, President George Washington named November 26 "a day of public thanksgiving" for the new government.

Many schools have special activities to celebrate the Constitution and the Bill of Rights.

You can celebrate Constitution Day, as well as Bill of Rights Day.

Constitution Day is September 17, which is the day the representatives at the Constitutional Convention signed the document. Bill of Rights Day is December 15. That's the date Virginia ratified the first 10 amendments, making them law. Have you been celebrating this important document?

The Miracle

We take it for granted now, but the Constitution was an amazing achievement for the young United States. George Washington said it was "little short of a miracle" that representatives from so many states could agree to this plan of government.

Washington would probably be amazed that the Constitution is still at work today. Back then, there were nearly 4 million US citizens compared to more than 300 million now. Though our borders have widened and numerous wars have been fought, the Constitution still guides our nation through it all.

Some of the articles of the US Constitution are broken down into parts called sections. The longest article—Article I—has 10 sections.

Glossary

ambassador: someone sent by one group or country to speak for it in different places

amendment: a change or addition to a constitution

American Revolution: the war in which the colonies won their freedom from England

Articles of Confederation: the agreement and set of laws that established the United States. An article is a piece of writing and a confederation is a group of independent states acting together.

constitution: the basic laws by which a country or state is governed

convention: a formal meeting for some special purpose

document: a formal piece of writing

expiration: the act of coming to an end

federal: having to do with the national government

ratify: to give formal approval to something

representative: a member of a lawmaking body who acts for voters

For More Information

Books

Krensky, Stephen. *The Constitution.* New York, NY: Marshall Cavendish Benchmark, 2012.

Labunski, Richard E. *James Madison and the Struggle for the Bill of Rights.* New York, NY: Oxford University Press, 2006.

Taylor-Butler, Christine. *The Constitution.* New York, NY: Children's Press, 2008.

Websites

Constitution for Kids: Articles and Amendments
const4kids.forums.commonground13.us/?p=21
Find easy-to-understand explanations for each part of the Constitution.

Constitution of the United States
www.archives.gov/exhibits/charters/constitution.html
Read the entire US Constitution and learn more fun facts.

Index